I Can Taste

Teacher's
Choice
Series

Lynda Laurance & Miriam Shaw
Anaheim, California

Photography by
Sheila Moran

Dominie Press, Inc.

These taste salty.

They are good.

These taste spicy.

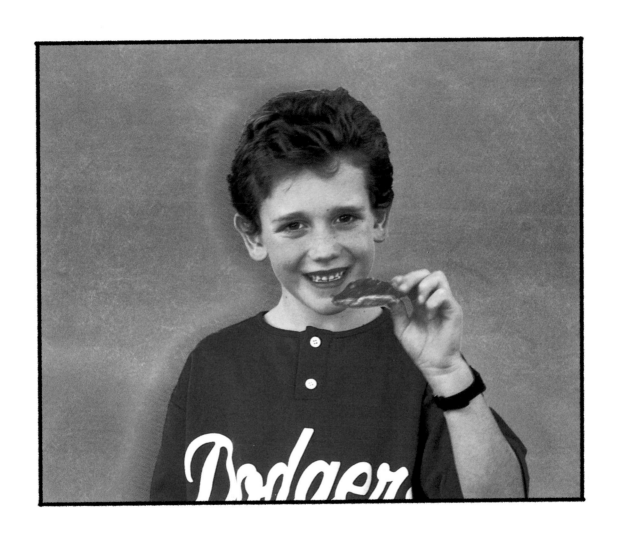

They are good.

These taste sweet.

They are good.

These taste sour.

They are good.

This tastes bitter.

This is not good!

The development of the *Teacher's Choice Series* was supported by the Reading Recovery project at California State University, San Bernardino. All authors' royalties from the sale of the *Teacher's Choice Series* will be used to support various Reading Recovery projects.

Publisher: Raymond Yuen
Series Editor: Stanley L. Swartz
Photographer: Sheila Moran
Cover Designer: Steve Morris
Page Design: Michael Khoury

Published by:

Dominie Press, Inc.

1949 Kellogg Avenue
Carlsbad, California 92008 USA

ISBN 1-56270-567-9
Printed in Singapore by PH Productions Pte Ltd.
2 3 4 5 6 IP 99 98 97